Rather than using real poop to test toilets, manufacturers use brown fermented beancurd. It looks—and can clog—just like the real thing!

Beaver poop often floats, because it contains so much undigested wood.

Sharks produce spiral poop.

When forced off their nests, eider ducks poop on their eggs to make them less appealing to predators.

Native American Lakota used the ashes from burned poop as toothpaste.

If food is scarce, young cockroaches can live by eating their parents' poop.

Food can remain in your body for up to two days before you poop it out.

On average, people use the toilet five times a day (once to poop, four times to pee).

During Operation Desert Storm in 1990, the U.S. military used toilet paper to camouflage their tanks.

Ancient Egyptian tombs had special toilet chambers for the pharaohs to use on their way to the afterlife.

Companies used to test their diapers by using mashed potatoes or peanut butter as a poop substitute.

One of nature's best ways to scatter the seeds of fruit trees is through the droppings of birds and animals that eat the fruit.

Scat, dung, and droppings are all general words for animal poop. There's also deer fewmets, cattle tath, otter spraints, cow flops or pats, buffalo bodewash, and bat guano.

The poop produced while people are fasting has little to no smell.

English king Henry the Eighth had a toileting stool covered with black velvet and studded with 2,000 gold nails.

During the American Revolution, English people jokingly hung portraits of George Washington in their bathrooms, since fear is supposed to help you poop.

Thomas Jefferson had an indoor bathroom at his home, Monticello, and servants hauled away his dirty chamber pots with a system of pulleys.

The ancient Romans had a goddess named Cloacina, who was in charge of toilets and sewers.

The average age for being toilet-trained in the United States is three years old.

Artist Michelangelo bathed some of his statues in donkey dung to make them look older.

In the ancient Roman city of Ephesus, rich citizens sent their slaves to the public bathrooms to warm up the cold marble toilet seats for them.

Many cultures used to try to get rid of freckles by rubbing dung on them.

One jokester in the 1920s made a toilet seat that played the National Anthem whenever people sat down—forcing them to stand up again.

The horses towing carts around Chinese cities must wear "butt bags" to keep the streets clean.

When they are upset, chimps who have been taught sign language indicate their frustration by making the sign for poop.

The TRUTH About POOP

by Susan E. Goodman

illustrated by Elwood H. Smith

PUFFIN BOOKS

Defecated to the ones I love—the Klein boys.   —S. E. G.

To my siblings, Jude, Dave, and Rich. Back in 1955, we endured a Michigan winter in a log cabin with an outhouse. Really.   —E. H. S.

ACKNOWLEDGMENTS:

It takes a lot of help to do a book like this one. Thanks to all the experts who gave me the straight poop on their specialties, including Jim Fuchs, formerly captain in the U.S. Air Force, Joyce Jatko of the National Science Foundation, Dr. Andrew Jones of York Archaeological Trust, Randy Morgan at the Cincinnati Zoo, Donald Rethke a.k.a. Dr. Flush, and Athos Bousvaros, Lenny Rappaport, and Ed Tronick of Children's Hospital Boston. A special thanks to Elizabeth Law for her sense of humor and editorial style, Teresa Kietlinski and Jim Hoover for their great layout, copyeditor Janet Pascal for keeping me from embarrassing myself, and Elwood H. Smith, whose illustrations are just so much fun.

—S. E. G.

PUFFIN BOOKS
Published by the Penguin Group
Penguin Young Readers Group, 345 Hudson Street, New York, New York 10014, U.S.A.
Penguin Group (Canada), 90 Eglinton Avenue East, Suite 700, Toronto, Ontario, Canada M4P 2Y3
(a division of Pearson Penguin Canada Inc.)
Penguin Books Ltd, 80 Strand, London WC2R 0RL, England
Penguin Ireland, 25 St Stephen's Green, Dublin 2, Ireland (a division of Penguin Books Ltd)
Penguin Group (Australia), 250 Camberwell Road, Camberwell, Victoria 3124, Australia
(a division of Pearson Australia Group Pty Ltd)
Penguin Books India Pvt Ltd, 11 Community Centre, Panchsheel Park, New Delhi - 110 017, India
Penguin Group (NZ), 67 Apollo Drive, Rosedale, North Shore 0745, Auckland, New Zealand (a division of Pearson New Zealand Ltd.)
Penguin Books (South Africa) (Pty) Ltd, 24 Sturdee Avenue, Rosebank, Johannesburg 2196, South Africa

Registered Offices: Penguin Books Ltd, 80 Strand, London WC2R 0RL, England

First published in the United States of America by Viking,
a division of Penguin Young Readers Group, 2004
Published by Puffin Books, a division of Penguin Young Readers Group, 2007

5 7 9 10 8 6

Text copyright © Susan E. Goodman, 2004
Illustrations copyright © Elwood H. Smith, 2004
All rights reserved

THE LIBRARY OF CONGRESS HAS CATALOGED THE VIKING EDITION AS FOLLOWS:
Goodman, Susan E., date-
The truth about poop / by Susan E. Goodman ; illustrated by Elwood H. Smith.
p.   cm.
Summary: A compendium of fascinating, weird, and gross facts about excrement.
ISBN: 0-670-03674-9 (hardcover)
1. Feces—Juvenile literature. [1. Feces.] I. Smith, Elwood H., date- ill. II. Title.
QP159.G665 2004 612.3'6—dc22 2003022547

Puffin Books ISBN 978-0-14-240930-5

Manufactured in China

Set in Bookman Medium

Contents

INTRODUCTION

We eat every day. And we talk a lot about food.
We get dressed every day. And we talk a lot about clothes.

WE POOP EVERY DAY, TOO.
But once we're old enough to do it by ourselves, we go into the bathroom and close the door. End of discussion.

It's time to take poop **OUT OF THE CLOSET**.
While we're pretending it doesn't exist, amazing things are happening in the poop department.

DID YOU KNOW...

You can be a **BATHROOM PICASSO**. Eating red meat will make your poop turn darker. Eating beets will make it red. Milk gives it a yellowish tinge, and blackberries can turn it green.

A skipper caterpillar is just an inch and a half long, but it can **SHOOT ITS POOP** a distance of six feet. This Brazilian caterpillar isn't practicing for basketball tryouts. The smell of its poop would tell hungry animals that dinner is near. So the caterpillar protects itself by flicking its feces as far away as possible.

Caterpillars aren't the only ones who should be careful. The navy suggests that people who are stranded at sea should store their **POOP IN THE LIFE RAFT**. Sharks can smell their prey's poop over a mile away.

KNOWING ABOUT POOP CAN SAVE YOUR LIFE.

And that's just the beginning. . . .

BIRDS DO IT, BEES DO IT

EVERYBODY POOPS

The simplest animals—like **JELLYFISH** and **SEA ANEMONES**—have a digestive system with only **ONE OPENING**. Their mouths do double duty—taking food in and pushing waste out. Clearly, having a system with a separate exit is a big improvement.

GROSS!

Animals with this "separate exit" use it in amazing ways. **TURKEY VULTURES**, for example, poop all over their own legs—and not because they have lousy aim. The evaporation of their mostly liquid poop keeps them cool on hot days.

CAMELS live in the desert and can't waste the precious water in their bodies on poop. Their droppings come out so dry that you could strike a match and burn them.

Unlike turkey vultures, **BATS** don't like to poop on themselves. But avoiding it isn't so easy when you hang upside down all day. So bats twist into special pooping postures to keep clean. (Some get dirty anyway. Fruit bats roost in trees, and only the group's "top" bats get to hang—clear and clean—in the highest branches.)

HOW MUCH?/HOW OFTEN?

RABBITS produce an impressive 500 pellets a day. Each of these brown balls is pretty small, but so is the rabbit.

HORSES can lift their tails and unload ten pounds' worth at a time—often without even breaking step.

Scientists recently found a chunk of fossilized **TYRANNOSAURUS REX DUNG** that weighed a whopping **16 POUNDS**. By studying this 17-inch, 65-million-year-old piece of paleo-plop, they learned that T. rex wasn't a careful eater. It barely chewed cow-sized dinosaurs enough to crush their bones before swallowing.

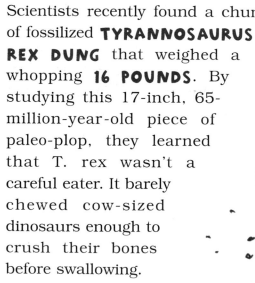

A **GOOSE** is a living poop factory. Food goes in one end and then . . . Geese poop, on average, once every 12 minutes.

SLOTHS, on the other hand, do everything slowly. They eat slowly. They digest their food ten times more slowly than a cow. They even poop slowly. Once a week, sloths, who do everything else in the treetops, slowly climb down to the ground to poop. They make the most of that trip. Sloths can poop out two pounds of waste in a single session—over a quarter of what they weigh.

While they're hibernating, **BEARS** don't poop at all. Their bodies create an internal plug made from feces, old cells, and hair that keeps them from pooping during their winter sleep.

DROPPED DROPPINGS

When we need to poop, we look for a bathroom. We're not the only ones. **ANTS** in New Guinea go to nubs on the branches of a special vine. As a reward to the plant for providing these perfectly shaped ant toilets, the ant poop rots into food for the vine's airborne roots.

LLAMA herds set up a "bathroom" area and wait their turns to use it. **WILDEBEESTS** grazing on the African plains also create a separate place to relieve themselves. This plan keeps fresh manure away from their dinner. It also fertilizes a new patch of grass for a future meal.

NAKED MOLE-RATS (which have been described as looking like hotdogs left in the microwave too long) live in eastern Africa in huge mazelike underground towns. Their special toilet chambers aren't designed simply to keep the rest of their burrows clean. Mole-rats regularly go in there to roll in their own poop. Strange taste in perfume? Not really. Mole-rat colonies have up to 300 members. The smell of their group's poop helps them distinguish between family and foe if a fight breaks out with another colony.

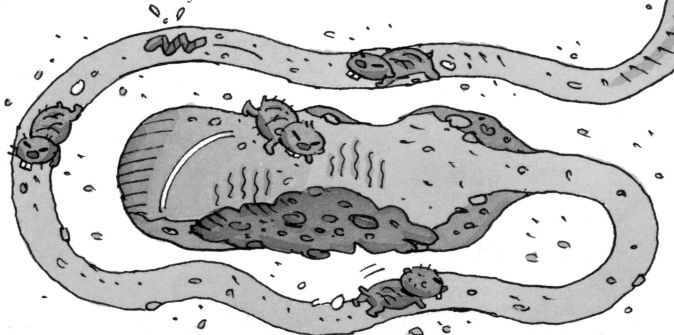

DUNG DISPATCH

Without telephones and email at their disposal, some animals use poop—at least the smell of it—to get their messages across.

The dung from a **MOTHER HORSE**, for example, says, "Here I am." The smell of her poop is one way her foal can find her.

A male **BLACK-FOOTED SALAMANDER's** poop also says, "Here I am"—but to a different audience. Female salamanders take a whiff to figure out what kind of food he has eaten. If he has eaten well, chances are he is strong and fit and will be a good father for their children.

The smell of **LION DUNG** would shout, "I'm here," too—something lions want to hide from their prey. That's why lions cover this evidence whenever they are on the prowl (a habit housecats carry over in their litterboxes).

When **WOLVERINES** are done feeding on a dead animal, they save the rest for later by pooping all over it.

What's the message? "This is mine, don't touch!" **AFTER THAT, WHO WOULD WANT TO?**

POOP WARFARE

It's a dog-eat-dog, bug-eat-bug world out there. And poop is often a **WEAPON** in the war. Some animals use it to trap dinner, others to avoid being dinner themselves.

It hardly seems fair—the **ASSASSIN BUG**, who loves the taste of termites, uses the termites' own droppings to trap them. It covers its back with termite poop and waits for the next poor termite looking for a toilet.

The **CRAB SPIDER** in New Guinea doesn't have to work so hard. Its coloring makes it look like bird droppings. When it's hungry, the spider sits on a leaf and splashes some extra white silk around to perfect its disguise as bird splat. The owlet moth that tries to sip a little salt from these droppings gets a deadly surprise.

Hunters aren't the only ones to use poop camouflage. The **TORTOISE BEETLE LARVA** starts eating as soon as it is hatched. It starts pooping shortly afterward, in golden strands, which it weaves into a shield. It munches on, hiding from enemies in its new poop-tent.

The **JAEGER** uses its poop as a weapon, not a disguise. Get too close to its nest of chicks and you'll find out how. Like any good fighter pilot, this seabird flies close to its target, then . . . bombs away!

THE ABCS OF ELIMINATION

BY PROCESS OF ELIMINATION

The eating part might be over when you leave the table, but you're hardly done with dinner. That's when **DIGESTION** kicks into gear. Your stomach starts churning, turning the food into nutritious goo. Most of it will be used as fuel to keep you going.

The rest is transferred to your body's **WASTE MANAGEMENT SYSTEM**. It travels through your intestines where it meets up with other trash your body wants to get rid of. It combines with extra water, old used-up cells, and unwanted bacteria. Lots of bacteria. On average, we poop out 100 billion bacteria a day.

The end of your intestines, the **COLON**, is like a waiting room. Poop gathers there until you feel that "urge to purge" and go to the bathroom. Generally, the more you eat, the more you poop. What you eat makes a difference, too. High fiber foods like vegetables create bigger stools. So does eating raw foods. Lots of meat and completely cooked foods produce smaller, darker ones.

BEFORE: 96 lbs

To know what's big and what's small, you have to know what is normal. On average, people produce about an **OUNCE OF POOP FOR EACH 12 POUNDS OF BODY WEIGHT**. So a 96-pound kid might flush away a half-pound of poop in a single session.

AFTER: 95½ lbs

HISTORY OF THE TOILET: PART I

In our part of the world, most people have flush toilets. But it took a lot of history to get this far. . . .

Long, long ago, people roamed the fields and forests and didn't have to keep things tidy. Once they started settling into **VILLAGES**, let alone cities, they had to figure out where to put their mess. From the beginning, smart people realized that using water to wash away waste was the goal. Even 4,500 years ago, one Asian culture poured water into their toilets so the contents would travel through chutes into an outside drainage system.

Medieval times in Europe were called **"THE DARK AGES"** for many reasons. Toiletwise, they remembered water, but forgot the plumbing. The toilets in some stone castles emptied out of tiny windows or long shutes into a hole in the ground—or a river if one was nearby.

Around this time, people said that London Bridge was built "for wise men to go over and fools to go under." Maybe the **PUBLIC BATHROOMS** located on the bridge had something to do with it. They emptied into the river below.

In 1596, **SIR JOHN HARINGTON** actually designed a flush toilet. But in 1596, buildings had no plumbing to bring in the water that makes a flush toilet flush. So people kept pooping in outhouses or inside in **CHAMBER POTS** and throwing the results out of windows onto city streets. And the flush toilet had to wait another few hundred years to become a welcome fixture in our bathrooms.

HISTORY OF THE TOILET: PART II

Once cities had sewer systems and bathrooms moved indoors (starting about 1850), the flush toilet's time had come. People like to think that British plumber **THOMAS CRAPPER** invented the flush toilet. He certainly had the best name for the job. And he did create a few of its improvements.

But many people pitched in to produce this all-important invention. One developed the first good **FLUSH MECHANISM**. Another made a **CERAMIC BOWL**, which was cleaner than the old wood or metal ones. Still another created a system to keep **OUTSIDE SEWER SMELLS** from traveling through the toilet into the house.

Toilets are still improving. Americans put **MOTORS** in some of them, adding power to each flush. The U.S. "Peacekeeper" reinforces Mom's lesson about putting the seat down—it's the only way to flush this model.

But the Japanese are the real winners of the Toilet Super Bowl. Press a button and some Japanese toilets make the sound of flushing water to hide more embarrassing sounds. Others have a kind of **EJECTION SEAT** for older people who can't stand back up without help.

One Japanese company makes a **"SMART TOILET"** that takes your temperature and blood pressure and can send this information to your doctor's office. One button on the **WASHLET TOILET** controls the temperature of the water that washes your backside. Another operates the blow-dry feature. This model is very expensive, but at least its owners save on toilet paper.

THE WORLD PRE-T.P.

There was a **WORLD BEFORE TOILET PAPER** and much of it wasn't pretty. Or comfortable.

Throughout history, wipers have reached for nearby objects. **LEAVES** were popular. **STONES** too, preferably smooth ones. Eskimos grabbed **MOSS** or **SNOW** depending on the season. Some people on the American coasts used **MUSSEL SHELLS**, which are actually a very convenient size and shape.

The ancient Roman version of toilet paper was a sponge on a stick sitting in a bucket of salt water. That may sound uncomfortable, but the Ouch Award goes to Spanish sailors who used the frayed end of **OLD ANCHOR CABLES**. Early Hawaiians are runners-up with **COCONUT HUSKS**.

And soon after the Pilgrims learned to grow corn, they figured out what to do with the **COBS**. Corncobs became the American wipe of choice for centuries. Kids were taught to start with red ones, then use a white cob to see if they should continue.

In 1391, the Chinese started producing **PAPER** for wiping purposes—but only for their emperors. These monarchs must have been very clean. Each sheet was three feet across.

The invention of the printing press created other papery possibilities. In a letter, the English nobleman Lord Chesterfield told his son to carry a **CHEAP BOOK OF POETRY** at all times. That way, he'd have something to read on the toilet and a good use for each page he finished.

When **DAILY NEWSPAPERS** became popular in the 1700s, ordinary people could afford to use paper. In the late 1800s, the pages of the Sears catalog hung on nails in outhouses across America, but first, moms tore out the pictures of women's undergarments.

TOILET PAPER ROLL CALL

By 1857, the printing press, bicycles, and baseball had already been invented. What was left? **TOILET PAPER!** So a New Yorker named **JOSEPH C. GAYETTY** produced the first TP in packs. Five hundred sheets of it sold for 50 cents. His idea was not a success. Evidently people weren't used to "wasting" an empty sheet of paper.

In 1890, the **SCOTT PAPER COMPANY** became the first ones to make toilet paper on rolls. Eventually the idea caught on—big time. A recent survey asked people what they'd want to have if stranded on a desert island. Almost half of them picked toilet paper over food.

Americans do like their toilet paper. On average, we use almost **9 SHEETS** per trip. And 20,805 sheets per year per person, which, when unrolled, would stretch three-quarters of a mile.

Americans use a lot, but Japanese women use more. On average, each one of them goes through about **TWO AND A HALF MILES** of the stuff a year.

Many people in India and Arab countries **DON'T USE TOILET PAPER** at all. They think smearing themselves with paper is a bad way to get clean. They **WIPE WITH THEIR LEFT HAND** instead and wash up with water. Unsurprisingly, they use only their right hand when eating.

WHERE DOES IT GO?

WHAT HAPPENS WHEN YOU FLUSH?

The water swishes out of your toilet into a pipe. If you live in a city, the pipe leads from your basement to a bigger pipe under the street. There, your poop and paper joins up with your neighbors'. Small pipes keep feeding into bigger ones until pipes up to 11 feet across carry rivers of watery waste to a **TREATMENT PLANT**. In Boston, for example, it takes more than 54,000 miles of sewers to do the job.

On its journey, your poop mixes in with everything from food that slipped down the kitchen sink to rain and leaves from the **STORM DRAIN**. At the plant, huge screens filter out big stuff like diapers and branches. Rocks and sand sink to the bottom of tanks and are carted away.

Poop and other solids settle to the bottom of the next tank and get a new name—**SLUDGE**. Some cities dry the sludge and **BURN IT**; others **DUMP IT** in landfills. Still others put it in an airless tank with a type of bacteria that finds it delicious. Whatever the bacteria leave behind is great for fertilizer.

In fact, when the city of Milwaukee, Wisconsin, realized this, they went into business.

Today, Milorganite (**MIL**waukee **ORGA**nic **NIT**rogEn) is a top-selling fertilizer for golf courses, which means that putting greens every-where are just a little greener thanks to the poop from Milwaukee.

EXTREME POOP

There are wild places on this planet far away from regular plumbing.
WHAT HAPPENS WHEN WE POOP THERE?

Disposal in the Amazon rain forest is not a problem, as one scientist discovered when he deposited a sample on the jungle floor. Within minutes, beetles and bees found this **TASTY TREAT**. Within a few hours, it had totally disappeared.

Getting rid of the stuff takes a lot longer at South Pole Station in Antarctica, where the average temperature is about –50°F. There, scientists use toilets placed over deep holes drilled into the icecap. The icecap is always moving seaward, so the poop and pee **GO ALONG FOR THE RIDE**. Today's wad of waste will reach the ocean in about 100,000 years.

High in the Andes Mountains, mothers carry
babies on their backs, wrapped in cloth slings. These tots
spend much of their day **LYING IN POOP** and pee and actually
GROW FASTER because of it. At 12,000 feet above sea level, it is cold, dry, and
harder to breathe. Being closed in with the waste creates a warm, humid
space. So the babies can put their energy into growing instead of staying warm.

In survival training, soldiers are
taught to **LIE ON POOP**, too.
Experts say that dry cowpats—
with a little give in the center—make a great
bed. Line them up and cover them with a poncho in
case one is still too "soft." Warmed up by a soldier's body,
they keep the heat all night long.

WASTE IN SPACE

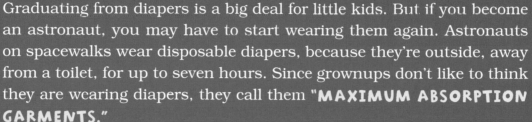

Graduating from diapers is a big deal for little kids. But if you become an astronaut, you may have to start wearing them again. Astronauts on spacewalks wear disposable diapers, because they're outside, away from a toilet, for up to seven hours. Since grownups don't like to think they are wearing diapers, they call them **"MAXIMUM ABSORPTION GARMENTS."**

Inside the ship, things are more problematic. In weightless conditions, anything loose—food scraps, stray pens, blobs of water—will float around the cabin. So good **WASTE DISPOSAL** is very important.

Take the rats, for example, that are part of science experiments. NASA wants the **RATS** to fly in space without their turds flying around the shuttle. During missions, steady streams of air flow through the rat cages. They push the poop and pee into waste trays and keep them there until the end of the flight.

Astronauts pee into a funnel, and gentle suction transfers the urine into a **HOLDING TANK**. The same kind of suction moves their poop into another tank. But pooping into a space toilet is complicated. Astronauts must swing bars across their legs to stay put.

Why? Gravity is one scientific law to worry about in space. **NEWTON'S THIRD LAW** is another. It says that every action has an equal and opposite reaction. When astronauts use their muscles to poop, they create a downward push.

The equal and opposite reaction? Without being held down, the astronauts would shoot **UP, UP, AND AWAY!**

USEFUL POOP

USEFUL POOP

We call it a waste product, but . . . Ancient Romans used pigeon poop to **BLEACH** their hair. And many expert gardeners insist that ZooDoo, made from elephant and rhino dung, is the **WORLD'S BEST FERTILIZER**.

What can you do with a pile of poop? **PLENTY.**

Today, doctors examine your poop to see if you have certain diseases. In the old days, they gave poop to you as **MEDICINE** instead. Hawk poop, lamb poop, **CROCODILE POOP**—they rubbed it on you, mixed it into food, or made a tea out of it to cure everything from dandruff to deafness.

Termites mix their poop with chewed-up wood to build the huge towers they live in. Secretary birds line their nests with **DRIED ZEBRA DUNG**. The Maasai, an African tribe, mix cow poop with ashes to make the walls of their huts. Luckily, the poop, once dried, doesn't smell at all.

The Bedouins of Qatar don't come across many toilets on their travels through the desert. Even today, they use dried camel pats **TO WIPE** their babies' bottoms.

AND THAT'S NOT ALL . . .

31

POOP CLUES

Police use **DOGS** to find missing people. Now scientists use them too—to sniff out the poop of wild animals. Scientists can learn a great deal about bears from their scat, for example, without ever bothering the animal itself. By looking at the DNA in poop, they can figure out which bear made it and which other bears it's related to.

PALEONTOLOGISTS learn about the past through fossils, including chunks of fossilized poop called coprolites. One scientist analyzed a piece made 20,000 years ago by a **GIANT GROUND SLOTH** in Nevada. By figuring out what this 1,000-pound animal ate, he also learned more about the climate back then. Now a **DESERT**, this area must have been very different then to grow the sloth's diet of grass, lilies, and grapes.

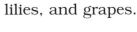

English scientist **ANDREW JONES** studied what Vikings ate by looking at their coprolites. But first he had to figure out which poop fossils actually belonged to the Vikings and not their pigs or dogs. To solve the problem, Dr. Jones put his own digestive tract to work. He copied the Vikings by eating lots of fish, bones and all. So did the dogs and pigs in his laboratory. Once he saw how leftover fish bones looked in his own poop versus fresh dog or pig poop, he could identify which of the fossilized stuff came from humans. The Vikings, by the way, also ate their share of beef and vegetables.

Humans aren't the only poop detectives. Small **WOLF SPIDERS** know when big, dangerous wolf spiders are near, by detecting chemicals in their poop. Then they move around much more carefully.

POOP POWER

Pioneers on the prairie didn't have trees or coal to burn as fuel. So settlers burned **DRIED BUFFALO CHIPS** to keep their houses warm.

Poop as fuel did not end with buffalo chips. In rural India, they use **"COW CHIPS."** Fresh cow manure is patted into round discs and stuck on walls to dry. As soon as it has dried enough to fall off the wall, it's ready to burn. India burns one quarter of all the dung its cows produce. That's fuel for 330 million people.

When poop gets old and breaks down without any oxygen around, part of it turns to gas. One out of every ten people on Earth burns this **POOP-GAS**, or biogas, as fuel. It actually makes a lot of sense. In the country of Nepal, for example, the poop-gas from two cows provides enough cooking fuel for a family of six.

Poop might even power our trips to **OTHER PLANETS**. NASA is studying how to burn food scraps, space garbage, and astronaut poop (along with regular fuel) to power a spaceship to Mars.

POOP AS FOOD

Cooking with poop is one thing but . . . **EATING IT**?

It might not sound so tasty to you, but many bugs search high and (mostly) low for a **DROPPINGS DINNER**. Up to one hundred different kinds of insects have been found dining on a single cowpat. Tumblebugs love the stuff. They roll their eggs in a ball of dung so their newly hatched babies will have a ready food supply.

When a dog chows down, however, it's usually to get a helping of bacteria. These tiny organisms move from the poop into the animal's gut. There, they help break down the new food that comes their way. That's why baby vampire bats polish off their parents' poop—they're **GOBBLING UP BACTERIA** needed to digest their special diet of blood.

Rabbits do it for a different reason. Just like cattle, rabbits eat plants that are really **HARD TO DIGEST**. A cow's stomachs let her bring food up again so she can break it down by chewing it twice. A rabbit can't do this. Eating its own poop gives the rabbit a second chance to get nourishment from its food.

POOP GAMES

When you want to **PLAY** outside, you might grab a ball or a Frisbee. The pioneers on the prairie had to make their own fun. Sometimes when gathering **DRIED BUFFALO POOP** for fuel, they competed to see who could toss the most chips into the wagon without breaking them.

Today, the rules are a little different at the annual World Championship **COW CHIP THROW** in Oklahoma. Chips must be at least six inches across. Wearing gloves isn't allowed. But licking your fingers for a better grip is legal. Contestants have two chances to throw these **"BROWN FRISBEES"** as far as possible. It's not all that far, by the way. The best throw ever is just about 16 feet.

Poop travels much farther at the **MOOSE DROPPING FESTIVAL** in Talkeetna, Alaska. There people buy numbered moose nuggets that are carried up 1,000 feet by weather balloon. At 6 p.m., a cord is pulled and it rains moose poop. The owner of the nugget that falls closest to the X drawn on the ground wins $1,000.

POOP PRESENTS

At the Moose Dropping Festival, people can buy **MOOSE POOP GIFTS** to bring home. Want a moose drop keychain? Or a mug with turds glued to its bottom? How about shiny brown buttons to sew on your sweater? Then there's the Poop Moose. Lift its tail and M&Ms drop out of its behind.

POOP ARTISTS in Alaska dry and paint moose droppings so they're hard and odor-free.

In Japan, they heat and press city sewage (a nice name for human poop) until it turns into something like brown stone. They use this **"METRO-MARBLE"** in necklaces and earrings.

A male **DUNG BEETLE** doesn't dress up the poop he gives to his girlfriend. He just uses his oversized fangs to make a big ball of it, one about 30 times her size. If she likes her gift, she climbs on top and he rolls off with her for a little romance.

DANGEROUS POOP

So far we've talked about poop as useful. Sometimes it's anything but. If you look up in most cities, pigeons are dripping white caps onto statues' heads, or adding polka dots to their robes. Pigeon droppings contain acid, which eats away at buildings, statues, wood, and car paint. Some cities are fighting back. London has outlawed selling pigeon food. And Venice has mixed birth control into its pigeon feed.

Pig manure is an even greater hazard—especially since there's so much of it (pigs produce four times more poop than humans). Some of its gases can eat through metal. And if a pig poops in a very hot place without enough air circulation, one gas in its poop (hydrogen sulfide) can actually kill it on the spot.

Certain scientists, however, discovered a way to use poop—at least the smell of it—to avoid killing anyone. Instead of firing guns to break up a crowd, a company called M2 Technologies suggests tossing in one of its **"POOP CAPSULES."** The smell is so intense that anyone nearby has to throw up—or run.

During World War II, "poop" really could kill. The British knew that German tank drivers fighting in the desert thought it was good luck to drive over camel dung. So they made **EXPLOSIVES** that looked exactly like the stuff. One pass over the poop—and the tanks were out of action.

German command ordered the drivers to avoid any dung, but superstitions are hard to give up. The Brits knew this and made mines that looked like dung squished by tank tracks. Drivers thought they were safe and . . . **BOOM!**

AFTERWORD—THE POOP ON POOP

There's a secret every nonfiction writer knows . . . research is fun. To write other books, I have paddled the Amazon River and shivered near the North Pole. For this one, I didn't do much hands-on research—thank goodness. But I did learn from personal experience how beets affect poop (page 4).

Mostly I read detailed, often scientific, books on the subject including:

- *Merde* by Ralph A. Lewin, published by Random House in 1999.
- *The RE/Search Guide to Bodily Fluids* by Paul Spinrad, published by Juno Books in 1994.
- *Cacas: The Evolution of Poo* by Oliviero Toscani, published by Evergreen in 1998.

Doing research can be a treasure hunt. No matter what question you have, someone somewhere has spent a lifetime thinking about the answer. Find that person and you've won the prize.

The treasures I found this time include Dr. Donald Rethke. He helped design space toilets for NASA (page 29)—and goes by the nickname Dr. Flush. Joyce Jatko at the National Science Foundation told me about poop at the South Pole (page 26). She also mentioned that sea urchins use toilet paper flushed into the sea from an Antarctic science center to drape themselves with as camouflage. I asked Dr. Andrew Jones if his experiment with poop (page 33) changed his eating habits. He said no, but he washes his hands much more often now. People who work with poop for a living have a great sense of humor.

IF YOU WANT TO DO A LITTLE RESEARCH OF YOUR OWN, YOU MIGHT TRY READING:

- *The Scoop on Poop* by Wayne Lynch, published by Fifth House in 2002.
- *Grossology* by Sylvia Branzei, published by Price Stern Sloan in 2002.

Or visit the website **www.theplumber.com**.

Rather than using real poop to test toilets, manufacturers use brown fermented beancurd. It looks—and can clog—just like the real thing!

Beaver poop often floats, because it contains so much undigested wood.

Sharks produce spiral poop.

When forced off their nests, eider ducks poop on their eggs to make them less appealing to predators.

Native American Lakota used the ashes from burned poop as toothpaste.

If food is scarce, young cockroaches can live by eating their parents' poop.

Food can remain in your body for up to two days before you poop it out.

On average, people use the toilet five times a day (once to poop, four times to pee).

During Operation Desert Storm in 1990, the U.S. military used toilet paper to camouflage their tanks.

Ancient Egyptian tombs had special toilet chambers for the pharaohs to use on their way to the afterlife.

Companies used to test their diapers by using mashed potatoes or peanut butter as a poop substitute.

One of nature's best ways to scatter the seeds of fruit trees is through the droppings of birds and animals that eat the fruit.

Scat, dung, and droppings are all general words for animal poop. There's also deer fewmets, cattle tath, otter spraints, cow flops or pats, buffalo bodewash, and bat guano.

The poop produced while people are fasting has little to no smell.

English king Henry the Eighth had a toileting stool covered with black velvet and studded with 2,000 gold nails.

During the American Revolution, English people jokingly hung portraits of George Washington in their bathrooms, since fear is supposed to help you poop.

Thomas Jefferson had an indoor bathroom at his home, Monticello, and servants hauled away his dirty chamber pots with a system of pulleys.

The ancient Romans had a goddess named Cloacina, who was in charge of toilets and sewers.

The average age for being toilet-trained in the United States is three years old.

Artist Michelangelo bathed some of his statues in donkey dung to make them look older.

In the ancient Roman city of Ephesus, rich citizens sent their slaves to the public bathrooms to warm up the cold marble toilet seats for them.

Many cultures used to try to get rid of freckles by rubbing dung on them.

One jokester in the 1920s made a toilet seat that played the National Anthem whenever people sat down—forcing them to stand up again.

The horses towing carts around Chinese cities must wear "butt bags" to keep the streets clean.

When they are upset, chimps who have been taught sign language indicate their frustration by making the sign for poop.